TopReaders

Pirates

Denise Ryan

Contents

Who were the pirates
and what did they do?
Let's find out.

Sea Robbers

Pirates were sea robbers.
They attacked ships and
seized their goods.

Pirates swung
on ropes to reach
this Spanish ship.

Pirate Map

Pirates attacked ships all over the world. Can you see where they worked?

NORTH AMERICA

Caribbean Sea

Ships and Flags

Each pirate ship flew its own flag. Crews on other ships had to look out for ships flying these flags.

Pirate flags were called Jolly Rogers.

Pirate ships were small and fast.

Treasure

Pirates forced the ships'
captains to give them gold,
silver, and other treasure.

They threatened the captains by taking prisoners.

Blackbeard

Blackbeard was a pirate who lived 300 years ago. He was armed with pistols and cutlasses.

cutlass

Blackbeard put burning strings in his beard to make himself look scary.

burning string

pistol

Women Pirates

Mary Read and Ann Bonny were pirates who attacked ships in the Caribbean Sea.

Ann Bonny

Mary Read

Women wore men's clothes. They were not expected to be pirates.

Pirates in Asia

Pirates in the China Sea rowed large junks. They attacked sailing ships.

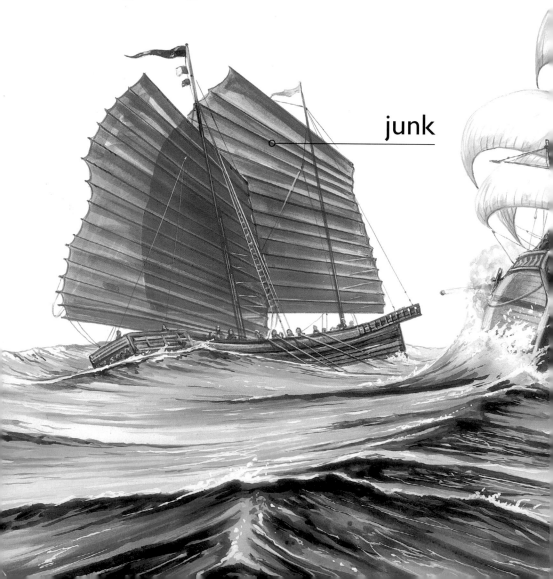

junk

The pirates captured the crews, then sank the ships.

Dangers

Ships could crash onto rocky shores. If pirates were waiting, they attacked the ship and killed the crew.

The pirates then stole the treasure.

Walking the Plank

Some cruel pirates forced
their prisoners to walk
the plank. The prisoners
drowned in the sea.

plank

Most pirates just tossed their prisoners overboard.

Punishment

Some pirates were caught and put on trial. They were sentenced to prison or to hard labor.

pirate

Some pirates were flogged and others were hanged!

Quiz

Can you match each picture with its name?

Blackbeard   Jolly Roger

junk   treasure